50 Dairy-Free Delights Recipes for Home

By: Kelly Johnson

Table of Contents

- Vegan Chocolate Avocado Mousse
- Dairy-Free Spinach and Artichoke Dip
- Coconut Milk Thai Curry Soup
- Almond Butter Energy Bites
- Cashew Cream Alfredo Pasta
- Roasted Red Pepper Hummus
- Quinoa Stuffed Bell Peppers
- Creamy Coconut Rice Pudding
- Chickpea Salad Sandwich
- Sweet Potato and Black Bean Chili
- Vegan Tofu Scramble
- Mango Coconut Chia Pudding
- Dairy-Free Pumpkin Pie Smoothie
- Creamy Broccoli and Potato Soup
- Almond Joy Energy Bars
- Avocado Lime Cilantro Dressing
- Vegan Mac and Cheese
- Blueberry Almond Oatmeal Muffins
- Coconut Milk Ice Cream
- Mediterranean Quinoa Salad
- Spicy Cauliflower Buffalo Bites
- Cashew Cheesecake Bites
- Dairy-Free Mushroom Risotto
- Peanut Butter Banana Smoothie
- Vegan Caesar Salad
- Sweet and Sour Tofu Stir-Fry
- Cucumber Avocado Gazpacho
- Almond Flour Banana Bread
- Dairy-Free Pesto Pasta
- Chocolate Coconut Bliss Balls
- Vegan Caprese Salad
- Creamy Butternut Squash Soup
- Maple Glazed Roasted Brussels Sprouts
- Raspberry Coconut Chia Jam
- Vegan Chocolate Chip Cookies

- Coconut Lime Quinoa
- Pumpkin Spice Smoothie Bowl
- Vegan Broccoli Casserole
- Dairy-Free Lemon Poppy Seed Muffins
- Thai Peanut Noodles
- Roasted Garlic and White Bean Dip
- Chocolate Avocado Truffles
- Sweet Potato Coconut Curry
- Vegan Blueberry Pancakes
- Dairy-Free Caesar Dressing
- Quinoa and Black Bean Stuffed Peppers
- Coconut Mango Sorbet
- Vegan Spinach and Mushroom Quesadillas
- Creamy Chocolate Avocado Pudding
- Roasted Vegetable and Lentil Salad

Vegan Chocolate Avocado Mousse

Ingredients:

- 2 ripe avocados
- 1/2 cup unsweetened cocoa powder
- 1/2 cup maple syrup or agave nectar
- 1/4 cup coconut milk
- 1 teaspoon vanilla extract
- A pinch of salt

Instructions:

Cut the avocados in half, remove the pit, and scoop out the flesh into a blender or food processor.
Add cocoa powder, maple syrup (or agave nectar), coconut milk, vanilla extract, and a pinch of salt to the blender.
Blend the ingredients until smooth and creamy. You may need to stop and scrape down the sides of the blender to ensure everything is well combined.
Taste the mousse and adjust sweetness or cocoa powder according to your preference.
Once the mousse is smooth and well mixed, transfer it to serving bowls or glasses.
Chill the mousse in the refrigerator for at least 30 minutes before serving to allow it to set and enhance the flavor.
Optional: Garnish with fresh berries, shaved chocolate, or a dollop of dairy-free whipped cream before serving.
Enjoy your indulgent and creamy vegan chocolate avocado mousse!

Dairy-Free Spinach and Artichoke Dip

Ingredients:

- 1 cup raw cashews, soaked in water for 2-4 hours or overnight
- 1 cup unsweetened almond milk
- 2 tablespoons nutritional yeast
- 1 tablespoon lemon juice
- 2 cloves garlic, minced
- 1 teaspoon onion powder
- 1/2 teaspoon salt
- 1/4 teaspoon black pepper
- 1 (14-ounce) can artichoke hearts, drained and chopped
- 1 cup frozen chopped spinach, thawed and drained
- 1/2 cup dairy-free mozzarella-style shreds (optional)
- Olive oil, for drizzling (optional)
- Chopped fresh parsley, for garnish

Instructions:

Preheat the oven to 375°F (190°C).

In a blender, combine the soaked cashews, almond milk, nutritional yeast, lemon juice, garlic, onion powder, salt, and black pepper. Blend until smooth and creamy.

In a mixing bowl, combine the chopped artichoke hearts, drained spinach, and dairy-free mozzarella-style shreds (if using).

Pour the creamy cashew mixture from the blender into the bowl with the artichoke and spinach mixture. Stir until all ingredients are well combined.

Transfer the mixture to a baking dish and spread it evenly.

Bake in the preheated oven for 20-25 minutes or until the dip is hot and bubbly, and the top is lightly golden.

If desired, drizzle a little olive oil over the top and garnish with chopped fresh parsley.

Serve the dairy-free spinach and artichoke dip with tortilla chips, sliced vegetables, or crusty bread.

Enjoy the creamy and flavorful goodness of this dairy-free twist on a classic spinach and artichoke dip!

Coconut Milk Thai Curry Soup

Ingredients:

- 1 tablespoon vegetable oil
- 1 onion, finely chopped
- 3 cloves garlic, minced
- 1 tablespoon ginger, grated
- 2 tablespoons Thai red curry paste
- 1 can (14 ounces) coconut milk
- 4 cups vegetable broth
- 1 tablespoon soy sauce or tamari
- 1 tablespoon brown sugar or coconut sugar
- 1 cup sliced mushrooms
- 1 red bell pepper, thinly sliced
- 1 carrot, julienned
- 1 zucchini, sliced into half moons
- 1 cup baby spinach leaves
- 1 cup firm tofu, cubed
- Juice of 1 lime
- Salt and pepper, to taste
- Fresh cilantro, for garnish
- Cooked rice or rice noodles, for serving (optional)

Instructions:

In a large pot, heat the vegetable oil over medium heat. Add the chopped onion and cook until softened, about 3-5 minutes.

Add the minced garlic and grated ginger to the pot, and sauté for an additional 1-2 minutes until fragrant.

Stir in the Thai red curry paste and cook for another minute, allowing the flavors to meld.

Pour in the coconut milk, vegetable broth, soy sauce (or tamari), and brown sugar (or coconut sugar). Stir well to combine.

Add the sliced mushrooms, red bell pepper, julienned carrot, and zucchini to the pot. Simmer the soup over medium heat for 10-15 minutes or until the vegetables are tender.

Gently stir in the baby spinach leaves, tofu cubes, and lime juice. Cook for an additional 2-3 minutes until the spinach wilts and the tofu is heated through.

Season the soup with salt and pepper to taste.
Ladle the Coconut Milk Thai Curry Soup into bowls and garnish with fresh cilantro.
Serve the soup as is or over cooked rice or rice noodles for a heartier meal.
Enjoy this flavorful and comforting coconut milk Thai curry soup!

Almond Butter Energy Bites

Ingredients:

- 1 cup old-fashioned oats
- 1/2 cup almond butter
- 1/3 cup honey or maple syrup
- 1/2 cup ground flaxseed
- 1/2 cup shredded coconut (unsweetened)
- 1 teaspoon vanilla extract
- 1/2 cup mini chocolate chips (dairy-free for vegan option)
- A pinch of salt (optional)

Instructions:

In a large mixing bowl, combine the old-fashioned oats, almond butter, honey (or maple syrup), ground flaxseed, shredded coconut, and vanilla extract.
Mix the ingredients thoroughly until well combined.
If the mixture seems too sticky, you can add more oats. If it's too dry, add a bit more almond butter or honey.
Fold in the mini chocolate chips until evenly distributed throughout the mixture.
Optional: Add a pinch of salt if you want to enhance the flavor.
Once the mixture is well combined, place it in the refrigerator for about 30 minutes. This will make it easier to handle.
After chilling, take small portions of the mixture and roll them into bite-sized balls using your hands.
Place the almond butter energy bites on a parchment paper-lined tray or plate.
Refrigerate the energy bites for an additional 15-30 minutes to firm up.
Once firm, transfer the energy bites to an airtight container and store them in the refrigerator.
Enjoy these almond butter energy bites as a quick and nutritious snack whenever you need an energy boost!

Feel free to customize the recipe by adding ingredients like chia seeds, chopped nuts, or dried fruit for added texture and flavor.

Cashew Cream Alfredo Pasta

Ingredients:

- 8 ounces fettuccine pasta (or pasta of your choice)
- 1 cup raw cashews, soaked in water for 2-4 hours or overnight
- 1 1/2 cups vegetable broth
- 3 cloves garlic, minced
- 2 tablespoons nutritional yeast
- 2 tablespoons lemon juice
- 2 tablespoons olive oil
- Salt and pepper, to taste
- Fresh parsley, chopped, for garnish (optional)

Instructions:

Cook the fettuccine pasta according to the package instructions. Drain and set aside.

In a blender, combine the soaked cashews, vegetable broth, minced garlic, nutritional yeast, lemon juice, olive oil, salt, and pepper.

Blend the ingredients until you achieve a smooth and creamy consistency. If the mixture is too thick, you can add a bit more vegetable broth.

In a large skillet over medium heat, warm the cashew cream sauce, stirring frequently. Allow it to simmer for 5-7 minutes until it thickens slightly.

Season the sauce with additional salt and pepper to taste.

Add the cooked fettuccine pasta to the skillet, tossing to coat the pasta evenly with the cashew cream sauce.

Cook for an additional 2-3 minutes, allowing the pasta to absorb the flavors of the sauce.

Remove the skillet from heat and garnish the Cashew Cream Alfredo Pasta with fresh chopped parsley, if desired.

Serve immediately and enjoy this creamy and dairy-free twist on classic Alfredo pasta!

Roasted Red Pepper Hummus

Ingredients:

- 1 can (15 ounces) chickpeas, drained and rinsed
- 1/2 cup roasted red peppers (about 2 peppers), drained
- 1/4 cup tahini
- 2 cloves garlic, minced
- 3 tablespoons olive oil
- 2 tablespoons lemon juice
- 1 teaspoon ground cumin
- 1/2 teaspoon smoked paprika
- Salt and pepper, to taste
- Optional: Pinch of cayenne pepper for heat
- Fresh parsley, chopped, for garnish
- Olive oil, for drizzling

Instructions:

In a food processor, combine the chickpeas, roasted red peppers, tahini, minced garlic, olive oil, lemon juice, ground cumin, smoked paprika, salt, and pepper.
Optional: Add a pinch of cayenne pepper for some heat.
Blend the ingredients until smooth and creamy. If the hummus is too thick, you can add a bit of water or additional olive oil to reach your desired consistency.
Taste the hummus and adjust the seasoning, adding more salt, pepper, or lemon juice as needed.
Transfer the roasted red pepper hummus to a serving bowl.
Drizzle with olive oil and garnish with chopped fresh parsley.
Serve the hummus with pita bread, vegetable sticks, or as a spread on sandwiches and wraps.
Enjoy the rich and flavorful roasted red pepper hummus as a delicious and nutritious snack or appetizer!

Quinoa Stuffed Bell Peppers

Ingredients:

- 4 large bell peppers, halved and seeds removed
- 1 cup quinoa, rinsed and cooked according to package instructions
- 1 can (15 ounces) black beans, drained and rinsed
- 1 cup corn kernels (fresh, frozen, or canned)
- 1 cup cherry tomatoes, diced
- 1/2 cup red onion, finely chopped
- 1/2 cup cilantro, chopped
- 1 teaspoon ground cumin
- 1 teaspoon chili powder
- 1/2 teaspoon garlic powder
- Salt and pepper, to taste
- 1 cup tomato sauce or salsa
- 1 cup vegan shredded cheese (optional)

Instructions:

Preheat the oven to 375°F (190°C).

In a large mixing bowl, combine the cooked quinoa, black beans, corn, cherry tomatoes, red onion, cilantro, ground cumin, chili powder, garlic powder, salt, and pepper. Mix well to combine.

In a baking dish, spread a thin layer of tomato sauce or salsa on the bottom.

Stuff each bell pepper half with the quinoa mixture and place them in the baking dish.

Drizzle the remaining tomato sauce or salsa over the stuffed peppers.

Cover the baking dish with aluminum foil and bake in the preheated oven for 25-30 minutes or until the peppers are tender.

If using vegan shredded cheese, uncover the dish, sprinkle the cheese on top of each stuffed pepper, and bake for an additional 5-7 minutes until the cheese is melted and bubbly.

Remove the stuffed bell peppers from the oven and let them cool for a few minutes.

Garnish with additional cilantro and serve.

Enjoy these delicious and nutritious quinoa stuffed bell peppers as a wholesome and satisfying meal!

Creamy Coconut Rice Pudding

Ingredients:

- 1 cup jasmine or basmati rice, rinsed
- 1 can (14 ounces) coconut milk
- 2 cups almond milk (or any non-dairy milk of choice)
- 1/2 cup granulated sugar or sweetener of choice
- 1 teaspoon vanilla extract
- 1/4 teaspoon salt
- 1/2 cup raisins (optional)
- Ground cinnamon, for garnish
- Shredded coconut, for garnish (optional)

Instructions:

In a medium-sized saucepan, combine the rinsed rice, coconut milk, almond milk, sugar, vanilla extract, and salt.

Bring the mixture to a gentle boil over medium heat, stirring frequently to prevent the rice from sticking to the bottom of the pan.

Once it reaches a boil, reduce the heat to low, cover the saucepan with a lid, and simmer for about 30-40 minutes, or until the rice is cooked and the mixture has thickened.

Stir in the raisins (if using) during the last 10 minutes of cooking.

Remove the saucepan from heat and let the rice pudding sit for a few minutes to cool and thicken further.

Taste the pudding and adjust the sweetness if necessary.

Serve the creamy coconut rice pudding in bowls, garnished with a sprinkle of ground cinnamon and shredded coconut if desired.

Enjoy this comforting and dairy-free dessert warm or chilled!

Chickpea Salad Sandwich

Ingredients:

- 1 can (15 ounces) chickpeas, drained and rinsed
- 1/4 cup vegan mayonnaise
- 2 tablespoons Dijon mustard
- 1 stalk celery, finely chopped
- 1/4 cup red onion, finely chopped
- 1/4 cup pickles, diced
- 1 tablespoon fresh lemon juice
- 1 teaspoon maple syrup or agave nectar
- 1/2 teaspoon garlic powder
- Salt and pepper, to taste
- Whole-grain bread or your preferred bread for sandwiches
- Lettuce, tomato slices, and any additional toppings

Instructions:

In a medium-sized bowl, mash the chickpeas with a fork or potato masher until they are mostly broken down.

Add vegan mayonnaise, Dijon mustard, chopped celery, red onion, pickles, lemon juice, maple syrup, garlic powder, salt, and pepper to the mashed chickpeas.

Mix all the ingredients until well combined and the chickpea salad has a uniform texture.

Taste the chickpea salad and adjust the seasoning according to your preference.

Refrigerate the chickpea salad for at least 30 minutes to allow the flavors to meld and the mixture to chill.

Toast or prepare your favorite bread for sandwiches.

Spoon the chickpea salad onto the bread slices, spreading it evenly.

Add lettuce, tomato slices, or any other desired toppings.

Top with another slice of bread to make a sandwich.

Serve your delicious and protein-packed chickpea salad sandwich for a satisfying and plant-based meal!

Sweet Potato and Black Bean Chili

Ingredients:

- 2 tablespoons olive oil
- 1 onion, chopped
- 3 cloves garlic, minced
- 1 large sweet potato, peeled and diced
- 1 red bell pepper, diced
- 1 jalapeño, seeded and minced (optional, for heat)
- 2 teaspoons ground cumin
- 1 teaspoon chili powder
- 1/2 teaspoon smoked paprika
- 1/2 teaspoon ground coriander
- 1 can (15 ounces) black beans, drained and rinsed
- 1 can (14 ounces) diced tomatoes, undrained
- 2 cups vegetable broth
- Salt and pepper, to taste
- Fresh cilantro, chopped, for garnish
- Avocado slices, for serving
- Lime wedges, for serving

Instructions:

In a large pot or Dutch oven, heat olive oil over medium heat.
Add chopped onion and sauté until translucent, about 5 minutes.
Add minced garlic and cook for an additional 1-2 minutes until fragrant.
Stir in diced sweet potato, red bell pepper, and jalapeño (if using). Cook for 5-7 minutes until the vegetables begin to soften.
Add ground cumin, chili powder, smoked paprika, and ground coriander to the pot. Stir well to coat the vegetables in the spices.
Pour in the black beans, diced tomatoes (with their juices), and vegetable broth. Bring the mixture to a simmer.
Reduce the heat to low, cover the pot, and let the chili simmer for 20-25 minutes or until the sweet potatoes are tender.
Season the chili with salt and pepper to taste.
Serve the sweet potato and black bean chili in bowls, garnished with chopped cilantro.
Top each serving with avocado slices and offer lime wedges on the side.

Enjoy this hearty and flavorful sweet potato and black bean chili as a comforting and nutritious meal!

Vegan Tofu Scramble

Ingredients:

- 1 tablespoon olive oil
- 1 block (14-16 ounces) firm tofu, crumbled
- 1 small onion, finely chopped
- 2 cloves garlic, minced
- 1 bell pepper, diced
- 1 cup cherry tomatoes, halved
- 2 cups spinach or kale, chopped
- 1/2 teaspoon turmeric powder (for color)
- 1/2 teaspoon cumin powder
- 1/2 teaspoon paprika
- Salt and pepper, to taste
- 1-2 tablespoons nutritional yeast (optional, for a cheesy flavor)
- Fresh herbs, such as chopped parsley or cilantro, for garnish (optional)
- Avocado slices, for serving (optional)
- Toast or tortillas, for serving

Instructions:

In a large skillet, heat olive oil over medium heat.
Add chopped onion and sauté until translucent, about 3-5 minutes.
Stir in minced garlic and cook for an additional 1-2 minutes until fragrant.
Add crumbled tofu to the skillet. Use a spatula to break it up and cook for 5-7 minutes until it starts to brown.
Add diced bell pepper and cherry tomatoes to the skillet. Cook for another 5 minutes until the vegetables are tender.
Sprinkle turmeric powder, cumin powder, paprika, salt, and pepper over the tofu mixture. Stir well to evenly coat everything with the spices.
Add chopped spinach or kale to the skillet and cook until wilted, about 2-3 minutes.
Optional: Stir in nutritional yeast for a cheesy flavor.
Taste the tofu scramble and adjust the seasonings if necessary.
Garnish the tofu scramble with fresh herbs, such as chopped parsley or cilantro.
Serve the vegan tofu scramble on toast, tortillas, or as desired.
Optional: Top with avocado slices for extra creaminess.
Enjoy this protein-packed and delicious vegan tofu scramble for a satisfying breakfast or brunch!

Mango Coconut Chia Pudding

Ingredients:

- 1/4 cup chia seeds
- 1 cup coconut milk (full-fat for creamier texture)
- 1 ripe mango, peeled and diced
- 1-2 tablespoons maple syrup or agave nectar (adjust to taste)
- 1/2 teaspoon vanilla extract
- Shredded coconut, for garnish (optional)
- Fresh mint leaves, for garnish (optional)

Instructions:

In a bowl, combine chia seeds and coconut milk. Stir well to ensure the chia seeds are evenly distributed.

Let the chia seed mixture sit for 5-10 minutes, stirring occasionally to prevent clumping. This allows the chia seeds to absorb the coconut milk and start thickening.

Add diced mango, maple syrup (or agave nectar), and vanilla extract to the chia mixture. Stir thoroughly to combine.

Taste the mixture and adjust sweetness if needed by adding more maple syrup or agave nectar.

Cover the bowl and refrigerate the mango coconut chia pudding for at least 2 hours or preferably overnight to allow it to set.

Before serving, give the pudding a good stir to redistribute the chia seeds.

Spoon the chilled pudding into serving glasses or bowls.

Optionally, garnish with shredded coconut and fresh mint leaves for added flavor and texture.

Serve the mango coconut chia pudding as a refreshing and nutritious breakfast, snack, or dessert.

Enjoy the tropical flavors and delightful texture of this delightful chia pudding!

Dairy-Free Pumpkin Pie Smoothie

Ingredients:

- 1/2 cup canned pumpkin puree
- 1 frozen banana, sliced
- 1 cup almond milk or other non-dairy milk
- 1/2 cup vanilla-flavored dairy-free yogurt
- 1 tablespoon maple syrup or agave nectar (optional, for sweetness)
- 1/2 teaspoon ground cinnamon
- 1/4 teaspoon ground nutmeg
- 1/4 teaspoon ground ginger
- 1/4 teaspoon vanilla extract
- Ice cubes (optional, for a colder smoothie)
- Whipped coconut cream, for topping (optional)
- Ground cinnamon, for garnish

Instructions:

In a blender, combine the canned pumpkin puree, frozen banana slices, almond milk, dairy-free yogurt, maple syrup (if using), ground cinnamon, ground nutmeg, ground ginger, and vanilla extract.

Blend the ingredients until smooth and creamy. If the smoothie is too thick, you can add more almond milk to reach your desired consistency.

Optional: Add ice cubes to the blender and blend again for a colder smoothie.

Taste the smoothie and adjust sweetness or spice levels if needed.

Pour the dairy-free pumpkin pie smoothie into glasses.

If desired, top each smoothie with a dollop of whipped coconut cream and a sprinkle of ground cinnamon.

Serve immediately and enjoy the seasonal and comforting flavors of a dairy-free pumpkin pie in smoothie form!

This smoothie is a perfect treat for fall or anytime you're craving the taste of pumpkin pie in a refreshing drink.

Creamy Broccoli and Potato Soup

Ingredients:

- 2 tablespoons olive oil
- 1 onion, chopped
- 2 cloves garlic, minced
- 3 cups broccoli florets
- 2 large potatoes, peeled and diced
- 4 cups vegetable broth
- 1 cup unsweetened almond milk (or any non-dairy milk)
- 1/2 cup raw cashews, soaked in water for 2-4 hours
- Salt and pepper, to taste
- Pinch of nutmeg (optional)
- Fresh chives, chopped, for garnish
- Croutons or toasted bread, for serving (optional)

Instructions:

In a large pot, heat olive oil over medium heat. Add chopped onion and cook until softened, about 3-5 minutes.
Add minced garlic and cook for an additional 1-2 minutes until fragrant.
Add broccoli florets and diced potatoes to the pot. Stir to combine with the onions and garlic.
Pour in the vegetable broth, bring to a boil, then reduce the heat to simmer. Cook for 15-20 minutes or until the vegetables are tender.
In a blender, combine soaked cashews and almond milk. Blend until smooth and creamy.
Once the vegetables are cooked, add the cashew-almond milk mixture to the pot. Stir well to combine.
Using an immersion blender, blend the soup until it reaches your desired smoothness. Alternatively, transfer the soup in batches to a blender and blend until smooth, then return it to the pot.
Season the soup with salt, pepper, and a pinch of nutmeg if desired. Adjust the seasonings to taste.
Continue to simmer the soup for an additional 5-10 minutes to allow the flavors to meld.
Ladle the creamy broccoli and potato soup into bowls.
Garnish with chopped fresh chives and serve with croutons or toasted bread if desired.

Enjoy this comforting and creamy dairy-free broccoli and potato soup as a nourishing meal!

Almond Joy Energy Bars

Ingredients:

- 1 cup almonds, raw or toasted
- 1 cup rolled oats
- 1 cup pitted dates
- 1/4 cup unsweetened shredded coconut
- 1/4 cup cocoa powder
- 1/4 cup almond butter
- 2 tablespoons coconut oil, melted
- 1 teaspoon vanilla extract
- 1/4 teaspoon salt
- 1/3 cup dairy-free chocolate chips
- 1/3 cup chopped almonds (optional, for extra crunch)
- Extra shredded coconut for topping (optional)

Instructions:

In a food processor, combine almonds and rolled oats. Pulse until they are finely ground.
Add pitted dates, shredded coconut, cocoa powder, almond butter, melted coconut oil, vanilla extract, and salt to the food processor.
Process the mixture until it comes together into a sticky, crumbly texture. If it's too dry, you can add a tablespoon of water.
Add dairy-free chocolate chips and pulse a few times until they are evenly distributed throughout the mixture. Optionally, add chopped almonds for extra crunch.
Line a square or rectangular baking dish with parchment paper, leaving some overhang for easy removal.
Press the mixture firmly into the prepared baking dish, ensuring an even layer.
Optional: Sprinkle extra shredded coconut on top and press it gently into the bars.
Place the baking dish in the refrigerator for at least 2 hours to allow the bars to firm up.
Once chilled, use the parchment paper overhang to lift the solidified mixture from the dish.
Cut the mixture into bars or squares of your desired size.
Store the Almond Joy Energy Bars in an airtight container in the refrigerator for freshness.

Enjoy these homemade energy bars that capture the flavors of an Almond Joy, providing a tasty and nutritious snack!

Avocado Lime Cilantro Dressing

Ingredients:

- 1 ripe avocado, peeled and pitted
- 1/4 cup fresh cilantro, chopped
- 1/4 cup olive oil
- 1/4 cup water
- 2 tablespoons lime juice
- 1 clove garlic, minced
- 1 teaspoon agave nectar or honey (optional, for sweetness)
- Salt and pepper, to taste

Instructions:

In a blender or food processor, combine the ripe avocado, chopped cilantro, olive oil, water, lime juice, minced garlic, and agave nectar or honey (if using).

Blend the ingredients until smooth and creamy. If the dressing is too thick, you can add more water a tablespoon at a time until you reach your desired consistency.

Season the dressing with salt and pepper to taste. Blend again to ensure the seasonings are well incorporated.

Taste the dressing and adjust lime juice, sweetness, or seasonings according to your preference.

Transfer the Avocado Lime Cilantro Dressing to a jar or container with a tight-fitting lid.

Store the dressing in the refrigerator for up to a week. Shake or stir before each use.

Use the dressing as a flavorful topping for salads, drizzle over grilled vegetables, or as a dipping sauce for various dishes.

Enjoy the zesty and creamy goodness of this avocado lime cilantro dressing!

Vegan Mac and Cheese

Ingredients:

- 2 cups elbow macaroni or pasta of your choice
- 1 cup peeled and diced potatoes
- 1/2 cup peeled and diced carrots
- 1/2 cup raw cashews, soaked in water for 2-4 hours or overnight
- 1/3 cup nutritional yeast
- 1/4 cup coconut milk or other non-dairy milk
- 3 tablespoons olive oil
- 1 tablespoon lemon juice
- 1 teaspoon white or yellow miso paste
- 1/2 teaspoon garlic powder
- 1/2 teaspoon onion powder
- 1/2 teaspoon turmeric powder (for color)
- Salt and pepper, to taste

Instructions:

Cook the elbow macaroni according to the package instructions. Drain and set aside.

In a pot, combine diced potatoes and carrots. Cover with water and bring to a boil. Cook until the vegetables are fork-tender.

In a blender, combine soaked cashews, nutritional yeast, coconut milk, olive oil, lemon juice, miso paste, garlic powder, onion powder, turmeric powder, salt, and pepper.

Add the cooked potatoes and carrots (reserve some cooking water) to the blender. Blend until smooth and creamy. If needed, add a little of the reserved cooking water to reach your desired consistency.

Taste the sauce and adjust the seasonings if necessary.

In a large mixing bowl, combine the cooked macaroni and the vegan cheese sauce. Stir until the pasta is evenly coated.

Serve the vegan mac and cheese immediately, garnished with additional nutritional yeast, black pepper, or fresh herbs if desired.

Enjoy this dairy-free and delicious version of mac and cheese!

Blueberry Almond Oatmeal Muffins

Ingredients:

- 1 cup rolled oats
- 1 cup almond flour
- 1/2 cup whole wheat flour
- 1 teaspoon baking powder
- 1/2 teaspoon baking soda
- 1/4 teaspoon salt
- 1/2 cup coconut oil, melted
- 1/2 cup maple syrup or agave nectar
- 2 flax eggs (2 tablespoons ground flaxseed mixed with 6 tablespoons water)
- 1 teaspoon vanilla extract
- 1 cup almond milk (or any non-dairy milk)
- 1 cup fresh or frozen blueberries

Instructions:

Preheat the oven to 375°F (190°C). Line a muffin tin with paper liners or grease with oil.

In a bowl, combine rolled oats, almond flour, whole wheat flour, baking powder, baking soda, and salt.

In a separate large bowl, whisk together melted coconut oil, maple syrup or agave nectar, flax eggs, vanilla extract, and almond milk.

Gradually add the dry ingredients to the wet ingredients, stirring until just combined. Be careful not to overmix.

Gently fold in the blueberries into the batter.

Divide the batter evenly among the muffin cups, filling each about 2/3 full.

Bake in the preheated oven for 20-25 minutes or until a toothpick inserted into the center of a muffin comes out clean.

Allow the muffins to cool in the tin for 5 minutes, then transfer them to a wire rack to cool completely.

Enjoy these wholesome and delicious blueberry almond oatmeal muffins for breakfast or as a snack!

Coconut Milk Ice Cream

Ingredients:

- 2 cans (28 ounces) full-fat coconut milk
- 3/4 cup granulated sugar or sweetener of choice
- 1 tablespoon cornstarch or arrowroot powder
- 1 teaspoon vanilla extract
- Pinch of salt

Optional Add-ins or Flavors:

- 1/2 cup shredded coconut
- 1/2 cup chopped nuts (e.g., almonds, pecans, or walnuts)
- 1/2 cup dairy-free chocolate chips or chunks
- 1/2 cup fruit puree (e.g., mango, strawberry, or raspberry)

Instructions:

In a saucepan, whisk together the coconut milk, sugar, cornstarch or arrowroot powder, vanilla extract, and a pinch of salt.
Heat the mixture over medium heat, stirring continuously until it begins to simmer.
Reduce the heat to low and continue to simmer for 5-7 minutes or until the mixture thickens slightly.
Remove the saucepan from heat and let the mixture cool to room temperature.
Once cooled, transfer the mixture to an airtight container and refrigerate for at least 4 hours or overnight to chill completely.
Pour the chilled mixture into an ice cream maker and churn according to the manufacturer's instructions.
If using any optional add-ins, fold them into the ice cream during the last few minutes of churning.
Transfer the churned ice cream to a lidded container and freeze for at least 4 hours or until firm.
Allow the coconut milk ice cream to sit at room temperature for a few minutes before scooping and serving.
Enjoy your homemade coconut milk ice cream on its own or with your favorite toppings!

Feel free to experiment with flavors and add-ins to create your own unique coconut milk ice cream variations.

Mediterranean Quinoa Salad

Ingredients:

For the Salad:

- 1 cup quinoa, rinsed
- 2 cups water or vegetable broth
- 1 cup cherry tomatoes, halved
- 1 cucumber, diced
- 1/2 cup Kalamata olives, pitted and sliced
- 1/2 cup red onion, finely chopped
- 1/2 cup crumbled feta cheese (optional for non-vegan version)
- 1/4 cup fresh parsley, chopped
- 1/4 cup fresh mint, chopped

For the Dressing:

- 1/4 cup extra-virgin olive oil
- 2 tablespoons red wine vinegar
- 1 clove garlic, minced
- 1 teaspoon dried oregano
- Salt and pepper, to taste

Instructions:

In a medium saucepan, combine the quinoa and water or vegetable broth. Bring to a boil, then reduce the heat to low, cover, and simmer for 15-20 minutes or until the quinoa is cooked and the liquid is absorbed.

Remove the saucepan from heat and let the quinoa cool to room temperature.

In a large mixing bowl, combine the cooked quinoa, cherry tomatoes, cucumber, Kalamata olives, red onion, feta cheese (if using), parsley, and mint.

In a small bowl, whisk together the extra-virgin olive oil, red wine vinegar, minced garlic, dried oregano, salt, and pepper to make the dressing.

Pour the dressing over the quinoa mixture and toss until all ingredients are well coated.

Adjust the seasoning to taste and add more salt or pepper if needed.

Chill the Mediterranean quinoa salad in the refrigerator for at least 1 hour before serving to allow the flavors to meld.

Before serving, give the salad a gentle toss and garnish with additional fresh herbs if desired.

Serve the Mediterranean quinoa salad as a refreshing and nutritious side dish or a light meal.

Enjoy the vibrant flavors of the Mediterranean in this wholesome quinoa salad!

Spicy Cauliflower Buffalo Bites

Ingredients:

For the Cauliflower Bites:

- 1 medium head cauliflower, cut into florets
- 3/4 cup all-purpose flour (or chickpea flour for a gluten-free version)
- 3/4 cup water
- 1 teaspoon garlic powder
- 1 teaspoon onion powder
- 1/2 teaspoon smoked paprika
- 1/4 teaspoon salt
- 1/4 teaspoon black pepper
- Cooking spray

For the Buffalo Sauce:

- 1/2 cup hot sauce (such as Frank's RedHot)
- 1/4 cup vegan butter or coconut oil, melted
- 1 tablespoon apple cider vinegar
- 1/2 teaspoon garlic powder
- 1/2 teaspoon onion powder
- 1/2 teaspoon smoked paprika
- 1/4 teaspoon cayenne pepper (optional, for extra heat)

Instructions:

Preheat the oven to 450°F (230°C). Line a baking sheet with parchment paper.
In a large bowl, whisk together the flour, water, garlic powder, onion powder, smoked paprika, salt, and black pepper until a smooth batter is formed.
Dip each cauliflower floret into the batter, ensuring it's well coated, and place it on the prepared baking sheet.
Lightly spray the cauliflower with cooking spray to help achieve a crispy texture.
Bake in the preheated oven for 20-25 minutes or until the cauliflower is golden brown and crispy, turning the florets halfway through.

While the cauliflower is baking, prepare the buffalo sauce. In a medium bowl, whisk together hot sauce, melted vegan butter or coconut oil, apple cider vinegar, garlic powder, onion powder, smoked paprika, and cayenne pepper (if using).
Once the cauliflower is done baking, transfer it to a large bowl and pour the buffalo sauce over the cauliflower. Toss until each floret is evenly coated.
Return the cauliflower to the baking sheet and bake for an additional 10-15 minutes until the sauce is absorbed, and the bites are crispy.
Remove from the oven and let the cauliflower buffalo bites cool for a few minutes before serving.
Serve with vegan ranch or your favorite dipping sauce.
Enjoy these spicy cauliflower buffalo bites as a tasty and plant-based appetizer or snack!

Cashew Cheesecake Bites

Ingredients:

For the Crust:

- 1 cup raw almonds
- 1 cup pitted dates
- Pinch of salt

For the Cashew Cheesecake Filling:

- 2 cups raw cashews, soaked in water for 4-6 hours or overnight
- 1/2 cup coconut oil, melted
- 1/2 cup maple syrup or agave nectar
- 1/4 cup lemon juice
- 1 teaspoon vanilla extract
- Pinch of salt
- 1/4 cup water (or more as needed for blending)

For Topping (Optional):

- Fresh berries, sliced
- Shredded coconut
- Drizzle of melted dairy-free chocolate

Instructions:

Line a muffin tin with paper liners or use a silicone muffin mold.
In a food processor, combine the raw almonds, pitted dates, and a pinch of salt for the crust. Process until the mixture sticks together.
Press the crust mixture firmly into the bottom of each muffin cup, creating an even layer.
In a high-powered blender, combine the soaked and drained cashews, melted coconut oil, maple syrup or agave nectar, lemon juice, vanilla extract, and a pinch of salt for the cashew cheesecake filling.
Blend on high speed until the mixture becomes smooth and creamy. If needed, add water gradually to achieve the desired consistency.
Pour the cashew cheesecake filling over the crust in each muffin cup, smoothing the tops with a spatula.

Optional: Top each cashew cheesecake bite with fresh berries, shredded coconut, or a drizzle of melted dairy-free chocolate.

Place the muffin tin in the freezer and let the cheesecake bites set for at least 4 hours or until firm.

Once set, remove the cashew cheesecake bites from the freezer and let them thaw for a few minutes before serving.

Enjoy these delicious and creamy cashew cheesecake bites as a delightful and guilt-free dessert!

Dairy-Free Mushroom Risotto

Ingredients:

- 1 1/2 cups Arborio rice
- 1/2 cup dry white wine
- 1 large onion, finely chopped
- 3 cloves garlic, minced
- 8 ounces mushrooms, sliced (e.g., cremini, shiitake, or button mushrooms)
- 4 cups vegetable broth, kept warm
- 1/2 cup nutritional yeast (optional, for a cheesy flavor)
- 2 tablespoons olive oil
- 2 tablespoons dairy-free butter
- 1 teaspoon thyme, dried
- Salt and pepper, to taste
- Fresh parsley, chopped, for garnish

Instructions:

In a large skillet or pan, heat the olive oil over medium heat. Add the chopped onion and sauté until softened, about 3-5 minutes.

Add the minced garlic and sliced mushrooms to the skillet. Cook for an additional 5-7 minutes until the mushrooms are tender and browned.

Stir in the Arborio rice and cook for 2-3 minutes until the rice is lightly toasted.

Pour in the white wine and cook, stirring constantly, until the wine is mostly absorbed.

Begin adding the warm vegetable broth to the rice mixture, one ladleful at a time. Allow the liquid to be absorbed before adding the next ladleful. Continue this process until the rice is creamy and cooked to al dente, which usually takes about 18-20 minutes.

Stir in the nutritional yeast (if using) and thyme during the last few minutes of cooking.

Season the mushroom risotto with salt and pepper to taste. Adjust the seasoning if necessary.

Remove the skillet from heat and stir in the dairy-free butter until it melts and makes the risotto even creamier.

Garnish the mushroom risotto with fresh chopped parsley.

Serve immediately, and enjoy this dairy-free mushroom risotto as a comforting and flavorful dish!

Peanut Butter Banana Smoothie

Ingredients:

- 2 ripe bananas, peeled and sliced
- 1 cup almond milk (or any non-dairy milk)
- 1/4 cup peanut butter
- 1 tablespoon chia seeds (optional)
- 1 tablespoon honey or maple syrup (optional, for added sweetness)
- Ice cubes (optional)

Instructions:

In a blender, combine the sliced bananas, almond milk, peanut butter, chia seeds (if using), and honey or maple syrup (if using).
Optional: Add ice cubes to the blender for a colder and thicker smoothie.
Blend the ingredients until smooth and creamy.
Taste the smoothie and adjust sweetness or thickness by adding more honey, maple syrup, or almond milk if needed.
Pour the peanut butter banana smoothie into glasses.
Optional: Drizzle a little extra peanut butter on top for garnish.
Serve immediately and enjoy this delicious and protein-packed peanut butter banana smoothie!

Vegan Caesar Salad

Ingredients:

For the Caesar Dressing:

- 1/2 cup raw cashews, soaked in water for 2-4 hours or overnight
- 1/4 cup water
- 2 tablespoons lemon juice
- 2 tablespoons nutritional yeast
- 1 tablespoon Dijon mustard
- 2 cloves garlic, minced
- 1 teaspoon capers
- 1/2 teaspoon vegan Worcestershire sauce
- Salt and pepper, to taste

For the Salad:

- 1 large head of romaine lettuce, chopped
- 1 cup cherry tomatoes, halved
- 1 cup croutons (ensure they're vegan)
- 1/4 cup vegan parmesan cheese (optional)

Instructions:

In a blender, combine soaked and drained cashews, water, lemon juice, nutritional yeast, Dijon mustard, minced garlic, capers, vegan Worcestershire sauce, salt, and pepper.

Blend the ingredients until you have a smooth and creamy Caesar dressing. If the dressing is too thick, you can add more water, a tablespoon at a time, until the desired consistency is reached.

Taste the dressing and adjust the seasonings if necessary. Add more lemon juice, salt, or pepper according to your preference.

In a large salad bowl, toss the chopped romaine lettuce, cherry tomatoes, and croutons.

Drizzle the Caesar dressing over the salad and toss until all the ingredients are well coated.

Optional: Sprinkle vegan parmesan cheese on top for added flavor.

Serve the vegan Caesar salad immediately as a refreshing and plant-based version of this classic dish.

Enjoy your vegan Caesar salad as a light and satisfying meal or a delicious side dish!

Sweet and Sour Tofu Stir-Fry

Ingredients:

For the Sweet and Sour Sauce:

- 1/4 cup soy sauce
- 3 tablespoons rice vinegar
- 2 tablespoons ketchup
- 2 tablespoons maple syrup or agave nectar
- 1 tablespoon cornstarch
- 1/2 cup water

For the Tofu Stir-Fry:

- 14 ounces extra-firm tofu, pressed and cubed
- 2 tablespoons cornstarch
- 2 tablespoons vegetable oil
- 1 bell pepper, sliced
- 1 cup pineapple chunks (fresh or canned)
- 1 cup broccoli florets
- 1 carrot, thinly sliced
- 2 cloves garlic, minced
- 1 tablespoon ginger, grated
- Cooked rice or noodles, for serving
- Sesame seeds and green onions, for garnish

Instructions:

In a small bowl, whisk together soy sauce, rice vinegar, ketchup, maple syrup or agave nectar, cornstarch, and water to make the sweet and sour sauce. Set aside.

In a large bowl, toss cubed tofu with cornstarch until well coated.

Heat vegetable oil in a large skillet or wok over medium-high heat. Add the tofu cubes and cook until golden brown and crispy on all sides. Remove the tofu from the skillet and set aside.

In the same skillet, add a bit more oil if needed. Stir in minced garlic and grated ginger, sautéing for about 1 minute until fragrant.

Add sliced bell pepper, broccoli florets, and carrot to the skillet. Stir-fry the vegetables until they are tender-crisp.

Pour the sweet and sour sauce over the vegetables and stir to combine. Cook for an additional 2-3 minutes until the sauce thickens.

Add the cooked tofu and pineapple chunks to the skillet. Gently toss everything together until well coated with the sauce.

Taste the stir-fry and adjust the seasoning if necessary.

Serve the sweet and sour tofu stir-fry over cooked rice or noodles.

Garnish with sesame seeds and chopped green onions.

Enjoy this flavorful and colorful sweet and sour tofu stir-fry as a delicious and satisfying meal!

Cucumber Avocado Gazpacho

Ingredients:

- 2 large cucumbers, peeled and chopped
- 2 ripe avocados, peeled and pitted
- 1/2 cup fresh cilantro, chopped
- 1/4 cup red onion, finely chopped
- 2 cloves garlic, minced
- 3 cups vegetable broth, chilled
- 1/4 cup lime juice
- 2 tablespoons olive oil
- Salt and pepper, to taste
- Optional garnishes: diced tomatoes, diced cucumbers, chopped cilantro, avocado slices, and a drizzle of olive oil

Instructions:

In a blender or food processor, combine the chopped cucumbers, avocados, cilantro, red onion, and minced garlic.
Add chilled vegetable broth, lime juice, and olive oil to the blender.
Blend the ingredients until smooth and creamy. If the gazpacho is too thick, you can add more vegetable broth to reach your desired consistency.
Season the cucumber avocado gazpacho with salt and pepper to taste. Blend again to ensure the seasonings are well incorporated.
Taste the gazpacho and adjust lime juice, salt, or pepper if necessary.
Transfer the gazpacho to a large bowl or individual serving bowls.
Chill the cucumber avocado gazpacho in the refrigerator for at least 2 hours to allow the flavors to meld.
Before serving, give the gazpacho a good stir.
Optional: Garnish each serving with diced tomatoes, diced cucumbers, chopped cilantro, avocado slices, and a drizzle of olive oil.
Serve the refreshing cucumber avocado gazpacho as a light and healthy appetizer or soup.
Enjoy the cool and creamy flavors of this delightful gazpacho on a hot day!

Almond Flour Banana Bread

Ingredients:

- 3 ripe bananas, mashed
- 3 large eggs
- 1/4 cup coconut oil, melted
- 1/4 cup maple syrup or honey
- 1 teaspoon vanilla extract
- 2 1/2 cups almond flour
- 1 teaspoon baking soda
- 1/2 teaspoon cinnamon
- 1/4 teaspoon salt
- 1/2 cup chopped nuts (e.g., walnuts or pecans), optional

Instructions:

Preheat your oven to 350°F (175°C). Grease a standard loaf pan or line it with parchment paper.
In a large bowl, mash the ripe bananas using a fork or potato masher.
Add the eggs, melted coconut oil, maple syrup or honey, and vanilla extract to the mashed bananas. Mix well until all the wet ingredients are combined.
In a separate bowl, whisk together the almond flour, baking soda, cinnamon, and salt.
Gradually add the dry ingredients to the wet ingredients, stirring until well combined. If using nuts, fold them into the batter.
Pour the banana bread batter into the prepared loaf pan, spreading it evenly.
Bake in the preheated oven for 50-60 minutes or until a toothpick inserted into the center comes out clean.
Allow the almond flour banana bread to cool in the pan for about 10 minutes, then transfer it to a wire rack to cool completely.
Once cooled, slice and enjoy this delicious and moist almond flour banana bread!
Store any leftovers in an airtight container at room temperature or in the refrigerator for a longer shelf life.

Dairy-Free Pesto Pasta

Ingredients:

For the Pesto Sauce:

- 2 cups fresh basil leaves, packed
- 1/2 cup raw pine nuts or almonds
- 2 cloves garlic, peeled
- 1/2 cup nutritional yeast
- 1/2 cup extra-virgin olive oil
- Salt and pepper, to taste
- Juice of 1 lemon

For the Pasta:

- 12 ounces (about 340g) gluten-free or regular pasta
- 1 cup cherry tomatoes, halved
- 1 cup baby spinach or arugula
- Optional: Dairy-free parmesan or nutritional yeast for topping

Instructions:

Cook the pasta according to the package instructions. Drain and set aside.
In a food processor, combine fresh basil, pine nuts or almonds, peeled garlic cloves, nutritional yeast, and a pinch of salt and pepper.
Pulse the ingredients until they are finely chopped.
With the food processor running, slowly pour in the extra-virgin olive oil until the pesto reaches a smooth consistency.
Add the lemon juice and pulse again to combine. Taste and adjust the seasoning as needed.
In a large bowl, toss the cooked pasta with the pesto sauce until well coated.
Gently fold in the halved cherry tomatoes and baby spinach or arugula.
Optional: Top the dairy-free pesto pasta with dairy-free parmesan or additional nutritional yeast.
Serve the pesto pasta warm or at room temperature.
Enjoy this dairy-free pesto pasta as a flavorful and fresh meal that's perfect for a quick lunch or dinner!

Chocolate Coconut Bliss Balls

Ingredients:

- 1 cup Medjool dates, pitted
- 1 cup shredded coconut (plus extra for rolling)
- 1/2 cup raw cacao powder or unsweetened cocoa powder
- 1/2 cup almonds or cashews
- 2 tablespoons coconut oil, melted
- 1 teaspoon vanilla extract
- Pinch of salt
- Water (as needed)

Instructions:

In a food processor, combine pitted Medjool dates, shredded coconut, raw cacao powder, almonds or cashews, melted coconut oil, vanilla extract, and a pinch of salt.

Process the ingredients until they come together into a sticky and crumbly mixture.

If the mixture is too dry, add water gradually, 1 tablespoon at a time, until the desired consistency is reached.

Scoop out tablespoon-sized portions of the mixture and roll them into balls using your hands.

Roll the bliss balls in shredded coconut to coat them evenly.

Place the chocolate coconut bliss balls on a parchment-lined tray or plate.

Chill the bliss balls in the refrigerator for at least 30 minutes to firm up.

Once firm, transfer the bliss balls to an airtight container and store them in the refrigerator.

Enjoy these chocolate coconut bliss balls as a delicious and energizing snack!

Feel free to customize the recipe by adding other ingredients like chia seeds, hemp seeds, or your favorite nuts for extra texture and nutritional benefits.

Vegan Caprese Salad

Ingredients:

- 4 large ripe tomatoes, sliced
- 1 pound (about 450g) vegan mozzarella cheese, sliced
- Fresh basil leaves
- Extra-virgin olive oil, for drizzling
- Balsamic glaze, for drizzling
- Salt and pepper, to taste

Instructions:

Arrange the sliced tomatoes and vegan mozzarella cheese on a serving platter, alternating them for a visually appealing presentation.
Tuck fresh basil leaves between the tomato and cheese slices.
Drizzle extra-virgin olive oil over the tomato and mozzarella slices.
Generously season the salad with salt and pepper to taste.
Finish the vegan Caprese salad by drizzling balsamic glaze over the top.
Serve the salad immediately as a refreshing and delightful appetizer or side dish.
Enjoy the vegan Caprese salad, celebrating the classic flavors of tomatoes, vegan mozzarella, and fresh basil!

Creamy Butternut Squash Soup

Ingredients:

- 1 large butternut squash, peeled, seeded, and cubed
- 1 large onion, chopped
- 2 carrots, peeled and chopped
- 2 apples, peeled, cored, and chopped
- 4 cups vegetable broth
- 1 cup coconut milk (or any non-dairy milk)
- 2 tablespoons olive oil
- 1 teaspoon ground cinnamon
- 1/2 teaspoon ground nutmeg
- Salt and pepper, to taste
- Optional garnish: roasted pumpkin seeds, drizzle of coconut milk, or fresh herbs

Instructions:

In a large pot, heat the olive oil over medium heat. Add the chopped onion and cook until softened, about 3-5 minutes.

Add the cubed butternut squash, chopped carrots, and apples to the pot. Stir to combine with the onions.

Pour in the vegetable broth, bring to a boil, then reduce the heat to simmer. Cook for 15-20 minutes or until the vegetables are tender.

Using an immersion blender, blend the soup until smooth and creamy.

Alternatively, transfer the soup in batches to a blender and blend until smooth, then return it to the pot.

Stir in the coconut milk, ground cinnamon, and ground nutmeg. Season with salt and pepper to taste. Adjust the seasonings according to your preference.

Continue to simmer the soup for an additional 5-10 minutes to allow the flavors to meld.

If the soup is too thick, you can add more vegetable broth or coconut milk until you reach your desired consistency.

Ladle the creamy butternut squash soup into bowls.

Optional: Garnish with roasted pumpkin seeds, a drizzle of coconut milk, or fresh herbs for added flavor and texture.

Serve the soup warm and enjoy the comforting and creamy goodness of this butternut squash soup!

Maple Glazed Roasted Brussels Sprouts

Ingredients:

- 1 pound Brussels sprouts, trimmed and halved
- 2 tablespoons olive oil
- Salt and pepper, to taste
- 2 tablespoons maple syrup
- 1 tablespoon balsamic vinegar
- 1/4 cup chopped pecans (optional, for garnish)

Instructions:

Preheat the oven to 400°F (200°C).

In a large bowl, toss the halved Brussels sprouts with olive oil, salt, and pepper until they are well coated.

Spread the Brussels sprouts in a single layer on a baking sheet.

Roast in the preheated oven for 20-25 minutes or until the Brussels sprouts are golden brown and crispy on the edges, tossing them halfway through the cooking time for even roasting.

While the Brussels sprouts are roasting, mix together maple syrup and balsamic vinegar in a small bowl.

Once the Brussels sprouts are done roasting, transfer them to a serving bowl.

Drizzle the maple-balsamic glaze over the roasted Brussels sprouts and toss to coat them evenly.

Optional: Garnish with chopped pecans for added crunch and flavor.

Serve the maple-glazed roasted Brussels sprouts as a tasty side dish.

Enjoy these sweet and savory Brussels sprouts as a flavorful addition to your meal!

Raspberry Coconut Chia Jam

Ingredients:

- 2 cups fresh or frozen raspberries
- 2 tablespoons chia seeds
- 2 tablespoons maple syrup or agave nectar
- 1 teaspoon vanilla extract (optional)
- 1/4 cup shredded coconut (optional)

Instructions:

In a saucepan, heat the raspberries over medium heat. If using frozen raspberries, you may need to thaw them first.

Mash the raspberries with a fork or potato masher as they heat, breaking them down into smaller pieces.

Stir in the chia seeds and continue to cook the raspberries for about 5-7 minutes, allowing them to soften and release their juices.

Add maple syrup or agave nectar to the raspberries and mix well.

Optional: Stir in vanilla extract for extra flavor.

Continue to cook the mixture for an additional 5-7 minutes, allowing it to thicken.

Remove the saucepan from heat and let the raspberry chia jam cool for a few minutes.

If desired, fold in shredded coconut for added texture and flavor.

Transfer the raspberry coconut chia jam to a jar or airtight container.

Allow the jam to cool completely before sealing the container and placing it in the refrigerator.

Refrigerate the jam for at least 2 hours or overnight to let it set.

Spread the raspberry coconut chia jam on toast, pancakes, or use it as a topping for yogurt or desserts.

Enjoy the delightful combination of sweet raspberries and coconut in this homemade chia jam!

Vegan Chocolate Chip Cookies

Ingredients:

- 1/2 cup coconut oil, melted
- 3/4 cup brown sugar, packed
- 1/4 cup granulated sugar
- 1/4 cup unsweetened applesauce
- 1 teaspoon vanilla extract
- 2 cups all-purpose flour
- 1 teaspoon baking soda
- 1/2 teaspoon salt
- 1 cup vegan chocolate chips

Instructions:

Preheat your oven to 350°F (175°C). Line a baking sheet with parchment paper.
In a large mixing bowl, whisk together melted coconut oil, brown sugar, granulated sugar, applesauce, and vanilla extract until well combined.
In a separate bowl, whisk together the all-purpose flour, baking soda, and salt.
Gradually add the dry ingredients to the wet ingredients, stirring until just combined. Be careful not to overmix.
Fold in the vegan chocolate chips until evenly distributed throughout the cookie dough.
Scoop tablespoon-sized portions of cookie dough onto the prepared baking sheet, leaving enough space between each cookie.
Bake in the preheated oven for 10-12 minutes or until the edges are golden brown.
Allow the vegan chocolate chip cookies to cool on the baking sheet for a few minutes before transferring them to a wire rack to cool completely.
Once cooled, store the cookies in an airtight container.
Enjoy these delicious vegan chocolate chip cookies with a glass of your favorite non-dairy milk or as a sweet treat!

Coconut Lime Quinoa

Ingredients:

- 1 cup quinoa, rinsed
- 1 can (14 ounces) coconut milk
- 1/2 cup water
- Zest of 1 lime
- Juice of 1 lime
- 1 tablespoon coconut oil
- 1/4 cup shredded coconut (optional, for garnish)
- Salt, to taste
- Fresh cilantro, chopped (optional, for garnish)

Instructions:

In a medium saucepan, combine the quinoa, coconut milk, water, lime zest, and a pinch of salt.
Bring the mixture to a boil over medium-high heat, then reduce the heat to low, cover, and simmer for 15-20 minutes or until the quinoa is cooked and has absorbed the liquid.
While the quinoa is cooking, heat the coconut oil in a small skillet over medium heat.
Add the shredded coconut to the skillet and toast it until golden brown. Stir frequently to prevent burning.
Once the quinoa is cooked, fluff it with a fork.
Stir in the lime juice, mixing it evenly with the quinoa.
Optional: Garnish the coconut lime quinoa with toasted shredded coconut and chopped fresh cilantro.
Serve the coconut lime quinoa as a flavorful and tropical side dish.
Enjoy this light and refreshing quinoa dish as part of a meal or on its own!

Pumpkin Spice Smoothie Bowl

Ingredients:

For the Smoothie Bowl:

- 1 cup canned pumpkin puree
- 1 frozen banana
- 1/2 cup unsweetened almond milk (or any non-dairy milk)
- 1/4 cup plain or vanilla-flavored vegan yogurt
- 1 tablespoon maple syrup or agave nectar
- 1 teaspoon pumpkin spice blend (or a mix of cinnamon, nutmeg, ginger, and cloves)
- Ice cubes (optional, for a thicker consistency)

For Toppings:

- Granola
- Chopped nuts (e.g., pecans or walnuts)
- Pumpkin seeds
- Dried cranberries or raisins
- Drizzle of maple syrup

Instructions:

In a blender, combine the canned pumpkin puree, frozen banana, almond milk, vegan yogurt, maple syrup, and pumpkin spice blend.
Blend the ingredients until smooth and creamy. If the smoothie is too thick, you can add more almond milk or a couple of ice cubes and blend again.
Pour the pumpkin spice smoothie into a bowl.
Top the smoothie bowl with granola, chopped nuts, pumpkin seeds, dried cranberries or raisins, and a drizzle of maple syrup.
Customize the toppings to your liking, adding your favorite nuts, seeds, or fruits.
Serve the pumpkin spice smoothie bowl immediately and enjoy the fall-inspired flavors!
Feel free to get creative with additional toppings like sliced bananas, coconut flakes, or a sprinkle of extra pumpkin spice for an extra burst of flavor.

Vegan Broccoli Casserole

Ingredients:

For the Casserole:

- 4 cups broccoli florets
- 1 cup carrots, shredded
- 1 cup vegan cheddar cheese, shredded
- 1 cup cooked quinoa or rice

For the Sauce:

- 2 cups unsweetened almond milk (or any non-dairy milk)
- 1/4 cup all-purpose flour
- 1/4 cup nutritional yeast
- 2 tablespoons vegan butter
- 2 cloves garlic, minced
- 1 teaspoon Dijon mustard
- 1/2 teaspoon onion powder
- Salt and pepper, to taste

For the Topping:

- 1 cup breadcrumbs (check for vegan-friendly option)
- 2 tablespoons vegan butter, melted
- 1/4 cup vegan Parmesan cheese (optional)

Instructions:

Preheat the oven to 375°F (190°C). Grease a baking dish.
In a large mixing bowl, combine the broccoli florets, shredded carrots, vegan cheddar cheese, and cooked quinoa or rice. Mix well and set aside.
In a saucepan, melt 2 tablespoons of vegan butter over medium heat. Add minced garlic and sauté until fragrant.
Stir in the flour and cook for 1-2 minutes to make a roux.
Gradually whisk in the unsweetened almond milk, nutritional yeast, Dijon mustard, onion powder, salt, and pepper. Continue to whisk until the sauce thickens.
Pour the sauce over the broccoli, carrots, cheese, and quinoa mixture. Mix until everything is well coated.
Transfer the mixture to the prepared baking dish, spreading it evenly.

In a small bowl, combine breadcrumbs, melted vegan butter, and vegan Parmesan cheese (if using).

Sprinkle the breadcrumb mixture over the casserole.

Bake in the preheated oven for 25-30 minutes or until the casserole is bubbly, and the top is golden brown.

Remove from the oven and let it cool for a few minutes before serving.

Serve the vegan broccoli casserole as a comforting and flavorful main dish or side.

Enjoy this delicious and wholesome plant-based casserole!

Dairy-Free Lemon Poppy Seed Muffins

Ingredients:

- 2 cups all-purpose flour
- 1/2 cup granulated sugar
- 1/4 cup brown sugar, packed
- 2 teaspoons baking powder
- 1/2 teaspoon baking soda
- 1/4 teaspoon salt
- 1 cup non-dairy milk (such as almond, soy, or oat milk)
- 1/2 cup vegetable oil (or melted coconut oil)
- 1/4 cup fresh lemon juice
- Zest of 2 lemons
- 1 teaspoon vanilla extract
- 2 tablespoons poppy seeds

For the Glaze:

- 1 cup powdered sugar
- 2 tablespoons fresh lemon juice
- 1 tablespoon non-dairy milk
- Zest of 1 lemon (optional)

Instructions:

Preheat your oven to 375°F (190°C). Line a muffin tin with paper liners.
In a large mixing bowl, whisk together the flour, granulated sugar, brown sugar, baking powder, baking soda, and salt.
In a separate bowl, combine the non-dairy milk, vegetable oil, fresh lemon juice, lemon zest, and vanilla extract.
Pour the wet ingredients into the dry ingredients and stir until just combined. Avoid overmixing; it's okay if there are a few lumps.
Gently fold in the poppy seeds.
Divide the batter evenly among the muffin cups, filling each about 2/3 full.
Bake in the preheated oven for 18-22 minutes or until a toothpick inserted into the center of a muffin comes out clean or with a few moist crumbs.
While the muffins are baking, prepare the glaze. In a bowl, whisk together powdered sugar, fresh lemon juice, non-dairy milk, and lemon zest (if using).

Once the muffins are done baking, allow them to cool in the tin for a few minutes before transferring them to a wire rack to cool completely.

Drizzle the lemon glaze over the cooled muffins.

Let the glaze set for a few minutes before serving.

Enjoy these dairy-free lemon poppy seed muffins as a delightful treat for breakfast or a snack!

Thai Peanut Noodles

Ingredients:

For the Peanut Sauce:

- 1/2 cup creamy peanut butter
- 1/4 cup soy sauce (or tamari for gluten-free option)
- 2 tablespoons rice vinegar
- 2 tablespoons maple syrup or agave nectar
- 1 tablespoon sesame oil
- 1 teaspoon grated ginger
- 1 clove garlic, minced
- 1/4 teaspoon red pepper flakes (optional, for heat)
- Water (as needed to thin the sauce)

For the Noodles:

- 8 ounces (about 225g) rice noodles or other noodles of your choice
- 1 tablespoon sesame oil
- 1 red bell pepper, thinly sliced
- 1 carrot, julienned or thinly sliced
- 1 cup broccoli florets, blanched
- 1/2 cup shredded cabbage
- 2 green onions, chopped
- 1/4 cup chopped peanuts, for garnish
- Fresh cilantro, for garnish

Instructions:

Cook the noodles according to the package instructions. Drain and set aside.
In a bowl, whisk together all the ingredients for the peanut sauce until smooth. If the sauce is too thick, add water gradually until it reaches your desired consistency.
In a large pan or wok, heat 1 tablespoon of sesame oil over medium-high heat. Add the sliced red bell pepper, julienned carrot, blanched broccoli florets, and shredded cabbage. Stir-fry the vegetables for 3-5 minutes until they are tender-crisp.
Add the cooked noodles to the pan, along with the peanut sauce. Toss everything together until the noodles and vegetables are evenly coated with the sauce.

Cook for an additional 2-3 minutes until the dish is heated through.
Divide the Thai peanut noodles among serving plates or bowls.
Garnish with chopped green onions, chopped peanuts, and fresh cilantro.
Serve the Thai peanut noodles immediately, and enjoy this flavorful and satisfying dish!

Feel free to customize the vegetables or add tofu or protein of your choice to make it a complete meal.

Roasted Garlic and White Bean Dip

Ingredients:

- 1 can (15 ounces) white beans (cannellini or navy beans), drained and rinsed
- 1 head of garlic
- 2 tablespoons olive oil
- 2 tablespoons lemon juice
- 1 teaspoon ground cumin
- 1/2 teaspoon paprika
- Salt and pepper, to taste
- Fresh parsley, chopped (for garnish)
- Optional: Red pepper flakes or cayenne pepper (for added heat)

Instructions:

Preheat your oven to 400°F (200°C).

Cut the top off the head of garlic to expose the cloves. Place the garlic head on a piece of aluminum foil, drizzle with a little olive oil, and wrap it in the foil.

Roast the garlic in the preheated oven for 30-35 minutes or until the cloves are soft and golden brown. Allow it to cool before handling.

In a food processor, combine the white beans, roasted garlic cloves (squeeze them out of the skins), olive oil, lemon juice, ground cumin, paprika, salt, and pepper.

Blend the ingredients until you have a smooth and creamy consistency. If the mixture is too thick, you can add a bit more olive oil or a splash of water.

Taste the dip and adjust the seasoning if needed. If you like it spicy, add red pepper flakes or cayenne pepper.

Transfer the roasted garlic and white bean dip to a serving bowl.

Garnish with chopped fresh parsley.

Serve the dip with pita bread, tortilla chips, vegetable sticks, or your favorite crackers.

Enjoy this flavorful and healthy roasted garlic and white bean dip as a delicious appetizer or snack!

Chocolate Avocado Truffles

Ingredients:

- 2 ripe avocados
- 1/2 cup unsweetened cocoa powder
- 1/4 cup maple syrup or agave nectar
- 1 teaspoon vanilla extract
- Pinch of salt
- Shredded coconut, cocoa powder, or chopped nuts (for coating)

Instructions:

Cut the avocados in half, remove the pits, and scoop the flesh into a bowl.
Mash the avocados with a fork or blend them in a food processor until smooth.
Add the cocoa powder, maple syrup or agave nectar, vanilla extract, and a pinch of salt to the mashed avocados.
Mix the ingredients until well combined, forming a smooth chocolate mixture.
Place the chocolate mixture in the refrigerator for at least 30 minutes to firm up.
Once the mixture is firm, scoop out small portions and roll them into bite-sized truffles using your hands.
Roll each truffle in shredded coconut, cocoa powder, or chopped nuts to coat them evenly.
Place the coated truffles on a plate or tray.
Refrigerate the chocolate avocado truffles for another 30 minutes to allow them to set.
Once set, transfer the truffles to an airtight container and store them in the refrigerator until ready to serve.
Enjoy these rich and creamy chocolate avocado truffles as a guilt-free and delicious treat!

Sweet Potato Coconut Curry

Ingredients:

- 2 tablespoons coconut oil
- 1 large onion, finely chopped
- 3 cloves garlic, minced
- 1 tablespoon ginger, grated
- 2 tablespoons red curry paste
- 1 teaspoon curry powder
- 1 teaspoon ground turmeric
- 1 teaspoon ground cumin
- 1 large sweet potato, peeled and diced
- 1 can (14 ounces) coconut milk
- 1 cup vegetable broth
- 1 cup broccoli florets
- 1 cup diced bell peppers (assorted colors)
- 1 cup cherry tomatoes, halved
- Salt and pepper, to taste
- Fresh cilantro, chopped (for garnish)
- Cooked rice or quinoa, for serving

Instructions:

In a large pot or deep skillet, heat the coconut oil over medium heat.
Add the chopped onion and sauté until softened, about 3-5 minutes.
Add the minced garlic and grated ginger to the pot. Sauté for an additional 1-2 minutes until fragrant.
Stir in the red curry paste, curry powder, ground turmeric, and ground cumin.
Cook for another 2 minutes to allow the spices to toast and release their flavors.
Add the diced sweet potato to the pot, stirring to coat it with the spice mixture.
Pour in the coconut milk and vegetable broth, and bring the mixture to a simmer.
Reduce the heat to low, cover the pot, and let it simmer for about 15-20 minutes or until the sweet potatoes are tender.
Add the broccoli florets, diced bell peppers, and cherry tomatoes to the pot.
Simmer for an additional 5-7 minutes until the vegetables are cooked to your liking.
Season the sweet potato coconut curry with salt and pepper to taste.
Serve the curry over cooked rice or quinoa.

Garnish with chopped fresh cilantro.
Enjoy this flavorful and comforting sweet potato coconut curry as a delicious and nourishing meal!

Vegan Blueberry Pancakes

Ingredients:

- 1 cup all-purpose flour
- 2 tablespoons sugar
- 1 tablespoon baking powder
- 1/4 teaspoon salt
- 1 cup non-dairy milk (such as almond, soy, or oat milk)
- 2 tablespoons vegetable oil
- 1 teaspoon vanilla extract
- 1/2 cup fresh or frozen blueberries
- Maple syrup, for serving

Instructions:

In a large bowl, whisk together the flour, sugar, baking powder, and salt.
In a separate bowl, combine the non-dairy milk, vegetable oil, and vanilla extract.
Pour the wet ingredients into the dry ingredients and stir until just combined. Do not overmix; it's okay if there are a few lumps.
Gently fold in the blueberries.
Preheat a non-stick griddle or skillet over medium heat. Lightly grease the surface with cooking spray or a small amount of oil.
Pour 1/4 cup portions of batter onto the griddle for each pancake.
Cook until bubbles form on the surface of the pancakes and the edges look set, then flip and cook the other side until golden brown.
Repeat until all the batter is used.
Serve the vegan blueberry pancakes warm with maple syrup.
Enjoy these fluffy and delicious blueberry pancakes as a delightful breakfast or brunch treat!

Dairy-Free Caesar Dressing

Ingredients:

- 1/2 cup raw cashews, soaked in hot water for at least 30 minutes
- 1/4 cup water
- 2 tablespoons lemon juice
- 1 tablespoon Dijon mustard
- 2 cloves garlic, minced
- 2 tablespoons nutritional yeast
- 1 teaspoon capers, drained
- 1/2 teaspoon Worcestershire sauce (ensure it's vegan)
- Salt and pepper, to taste
- 1/3 cup extra-virgin olive oil

Instructions:

In a blender, combine the soaked cashews, water, lemon juice, Dijon mustard, minced garlic, nutritional yeast, capers, Worcestershire sauce, salt, and pepper. Blend the ingredients until smooth and creamy.

While the blender is running, gradually drizzle in the extra-virgin olive oil until the dressing is emulsified and well combined.

Taste the dressing and adjust the seasoning if needed, adding more salt, pepper, or lemon juice to suit your preferences.

Transfer the dairy-free Caesar dressing to a jar or airtight container.

Store the dressing in the refrigerator for at least 1-2 hours before using to allow the flavors to meld.

Shake or stir the dressing well before serving.

Use the dairy-free Caesar dressing on salads, as a dip for veggies, or in any recipe that calls for Caesar dressing.

Enjoy the rich and creamy flavor of this dairy-free Caesar dressing without any animal products!

Quinoa and Black Bean Stuffed Peppers

Ingredients:

- 4 large bell peppers, halved and seeds removed
- 1 cup quinoa, rinsed
- 2 cups vegetable broth or water
- 1 can (15 ounces) black beans, drained and rinsed
- 1 cup corn kernels (fresh or frozen)
- 1 cup diced tomatoes
- 1 cup red onion, finely chopped
- 1 cup bell pepper, diced (from the tops of the peppers)
- 2 cloves garlic, minced
- 1 teaspoon ground cumin
- 1 teaspoon chili powder
- Salt and pepper, to taste
- 1 cup vegan cheese, shredded (optional)
- Fresh cilantro, chopped (for garnish)

Instructions:

Preheat the oven to 375°F (190°C).

In a medium saucepan, combine the quinoa and vegetable broth or water. Bring to a boil, then reduce the heat to low, cover, and simmer for 15-20 minutes or until the quinoa is cooked and the liquid is absorbed.

In a large mixing bowl, combine the cooked quinoa, black beans, corn, diced tomatoes, red onion, diced bell pepper (from the tops), minced garlic, ground cumin, chili powder, salt, and pepper. Mix well to combine.

Place the halved bell peppers in a baking dish.

Stuff each pepper half with the quinoa and black bean mixture, pressing down lightly to pack the filling.

If using vegan cheese, sprinkle it over the top of each stuffed pepper.

Cover the baking dish with aluminum foil.

Bake in the preheated oven for 25-30 minutes or until the peppers are tender.

Remove the foil and bake for an additional 5-10 minutes until the cheese (if using) is melted and bubbly.

Garnish the quinoa and black bean stuffed peppers with chopped fresh cilantro.

Serve the stuffed peppers warm and enjoy this wholesome and flavorful dish!

Feel free to customize the recipe by adding your favorite toppings like avocado, salsa, or a drizzle of vegan sour cream.

Coconut Mango Sorbet

Ingredients:

- 3 cups ripe mango, peeled and diced
- 1 can (13.5 ounces) coconut milk
- 1/2 cup granulated sugar (adjust to taste)
- 1 tablespoon lime juice
- Pinch of salt

Instructions:

Place the diced mango in a blender or food processor.
Add the coconut milk, granulated sugar, lime juice, and a pinch of salt to the blender.
Blend the ingredients until smooth and well combined.
Taste the mixture and adjust the sweetness by adding more sugar if needed.
Pour the mango coconut mixture into a shallow dish or an ice cream maker.
If using a shallow dish, cover it with plastic wrap. Place the mixture in the freezer.
If using an ice cream maker, follow the manufacturer's instructions for churning.
If using a shallow dish, every 30 minutes, remove the dish from the freezer and stir the sorbet with a fork to break up any ice crystals. Repeat this process for 2-3 hours or until the sorbet reaches a firm and scoopable consistency.
Once the coconut mango sorbet is frozen to your liking, scoop it into bowls or cones.
Garnish with fresh mango slices or mint leaves if desired.
Serve immediately and enjoy this refreshing coconut mango sorbet as a delightful frozen treat!

Vegan Spinach and Mushroom Quesadillas

Ingredients:

- 1 tablespoon olive oil
- 1 small onion, finely chopped
- 2 cloves garlic, minced
- 8 ounces (about 227g) mushrooms, sliced
- 4 cups fresh spinach, chopped
- Salt and pepper, to taste
- 4 large flour tortillas
- 1 cup vegan cheese, shredded
- 1 ripe avocado, sliced
- Salsa, for serving
- Vegan sour cream, for serving (optional)

Instructions:

In a large skillet, heat olive oil over medium heat.
Add the chopped onion and cook until softened, about 3-5 minutes.
Add the minced garlic and sliced mushrooms to the skillet. Cook until the mushrooms release their moisture and become golden brown.
Stir in the chopped spinach and cook until wilted. Season with salt and pepper to taste.
Remove the skillet from the heat and set aside.
Place a tortilla on a flat surface. Spread a portion of the mushroom and spinach mixture evenly over one half of the tortilla.
Sprinkle a generous amount of vegan cheese over the mushroom and spinach mixture.
Fold the other half of the tortilla over the filling, creating a half-moon shape.
Repeat the process with the remaining tortillas and filling.
In a large skillet or griddle, heat each quesadilla over medium heat until the tortillas are golden brown and the cheese is melted. This takes about 2-3 minutes per side.
Once cooked, remove the quesadillas from the skillet and slice them into wedges.
Serve the vegan spinach and mushroom quesadillas with sliced avocado, salsa, and vegan sour cream if desired.
Enjoy these flavorful and satisfying quesadillas as a delicious plant-based meal!

Creamy Chocolate Avocado Pudding

Ingredients:

- 2 ripe avocados
- 1/2 cup cocoa powder
- 1/2 cup maple syrup or agave nectar
- 1/3 cup non-dairy milk (such as almond, soy, or oat milk)
- 1 teaspoon vanilla extract
- Pinch of salt
- Optional toppings: Fresh berries, sliced bananas, chopped nuts, or coconut flakes

Instructions:

Cut the avocados in half, remove the pits, and scoop the flesh into a blender or food processor.

Add the cocoa powder, maple syrup or agave nectar, non-dairy milk, vanilla extract, and a pinch of salt to the blender.

Blend the ingredients until smooth and creamy. You may need to stop and scrape down the sides of the blender or food processor to ensure everything is well incorporated.

Taste the pudding and adjust the sweetness if needed by adding more maple syrup or agave nectar.

Once the pudding is smooth and sweetened to your liking, transfer it to serving bowls or glasses.

Refrigerate the chocolate avocado pudding for at least 1-2 hours to allow it to chill and thicken.

Before serving, give the pudding a quick stir.

Optionally, top the creamy chocolate avocado pudding with fresh berries, sliced bananas, chopped nuts, or coconut flakes.

Serve the pudding chilled and enjoy this rich and indulgent chocolate treat!

Roasted Vegetable and Lentil Salad

Ingredients:

For the Salad:

- 1 cup dry green or brown lentils
- 3 cups mixed vegetables (e.g., cherry tomatoes, bell peppers, zucchini, red onion, carrots), chopped
- 2 tablespoons olive oil
- Salt and pepper, to taste
- 6 cups mixed salad greens (e.g., spinach, arugula, kale)

For the Dressing:

- 3 tablespoons balsamic vinegar
- 2 tablespoons olive oil
- 1 tablespoon Dijon mustard
- 1 clove garlic, minced
- Salt and pepper, to taste

Optional Additions:

- 1/2 cup crumbled feta or vegan feta (optional)
- Fresh herbs (e.g., parsley, basil), chopped

Instructions:

Preheat the oven to 400°F (200°C).
Rinse the lentils under cold water. In a medium saucepan, combine the lentils with 3 cups of water. Bring to a boil, then reduce the heat to low, cover, and simmer for about 20-25 minutes or until the lentils are tender but not mushy. Drain any excess water and set aside.
In a large mixing bowl, toss the chopped vegetables with olive oil, salt, and pepper.
Spread the vegetables in a single layer on a baking sheet.

Roast the vegetables in the preheated oven for 20-25 minutes or until they are tender and slightly caramelized. Stir them halfway through the roasting time for even cooking.

While the vegetables are roasting, whisk together the balsamic vinegar, olive oil, Dijon mustard, minced garlic, salt, and pepper to make the dressing.

In a large salad bowl, combine the cooked lentils, roasted vegetables, and mixed salad greens.

Drizzle the dressing over the salad and toss everything gently to coat.

If desired, add crumbled feta or vegan feta and fresh herbs to the salad.

Serve the roasted vegetable and lentil salad as a hearty and nutritious meal.

Enjoy the combination of earthy lentils, roasted vegetables, and flavorful dressing in this satisfying salad!